Dear Parents,

Welcome to the Scholastic Reader series. We have taken over 80 years of experience with teachers, parents, and children and put it into a program that is designed to match your child's interests and skills.

Level 1—Short sentences and stories made up of words kids can sound out using their phonics skills and words that are important to remember.

Level 2—Longer sentences and stories with words kids need to know and new "big" words that they will want to know.

Level 3—From sentences to paragraphs to longer stories, these books have large "chunks" of texts and are made up of a rich vocabulary.

Level 4—First chapter books with more words and fewer pictures.

It is important that children learn to read well enough to succeed in school and beyond. Here are ideas for reading this book with your child:

- Look at the book together. Encourage your child to read the title and make a prediction about the story.
- Read the book together. Encourage your child to sound out words when appropriate. When your child struggles, you can help by providing the word.
- Encourage your child to retell the story. This is a great way to check for comprehension.
- Have your child take the fluency test on the last page to check progress.

Scholastic Readers are designed to support your child's efforts to learn how to read at every age and every stage. Enjoy helping your child learn to read and love to read.

—**Francie Alexander**
Chief Education Officer
Scholastic Education

PHOTO CREDITS

page 4 Schomburg Center for Research in Black Culture, NYPL
page 8 *Frank Leslie's*, April 16, 1870
page 9 Long Island Historical Society
page 11 Denver Public Library
page 12 National Portrait Gallery, Smithsonian Institution © Dr. Donald Polk
page 17 Simpson College, painting by Emily Vermillion, "Henry A. Wallace and George Washington Carver," oil on canvas, 1987
page 19 National Portrait Gallery, Smithsonian Instition
page 21 Corbis/Bettman
pages 22, 27 courtesy, Prints and Photographs Collection, Moorland-Spingarn Research Center, Howard University
page 28 Corbis
page 32 Schomburg Center for Research in Black Culture, NYPL
page 37 Corbis
page 39 Corbis/Stephanie Maze
pages 40, 48 right Nuclear Regulatory Commission
page 45 courtesy, New Jersey Institute of Technology
pages 46, 48 left Corbis

Produced by Just Us Books, Inc.
356 Glenwood Avenue
East Orange, NJ 07017

Library of Congress Cataloging-in-Publication Data is available.

ISBN 0-590-48031-6

10   07

Printed in the U.S.A.   23
First Scholastic printing, February 2000

Five Brilliant Scientists

by Lynda Jones
Illustrated by Ron Garnett

Scholastic Reader — Level 4

SCHOLASTIC INC.
New York   Toronto   London   Auckland   Sydney
Mexico City   New Delhi   Hong Kong   Buenos Aires

Susan McKinney Steward

BORN 1847 - DIED 1918

Caring Children's Doctor

In March 1847, in Brooklyn, New York, the Smith family gathered for a celebration. Sylvanus and Anne Smith welcomed their seventh child—a beautiful baby girl named Susan Maria Smith.

Susan would grow up to do great things. She would become the first Black female doctor in New York State.

No one's sure why Susan decided to become a doctor. Some say she became interested in medicine because her niece had become very ill. Susan helped take care of her. But the girl was so ill that she died. Soon after, Susan announced to her family, "I'm going to become a doctor."

Women doctors were very rare in those days. *Black* women doctors were even more rare. There were only two in the entire country! Many men at that time didn't believe women should become doctors. But Susan said stubbornly, "*I* can do it."

In 1867, when she was 20 years old, Susan entered the New York Medical College and Hospital for Women in New York City. The college taught *homeopathy*, a special type of medicine that treated patients with drugs containing some of the same germs that had made the patients ill.

Homeopathy was introduced to the United States from England in 1825. Many people did not trust this type of medicine because it was so different. But Susan was fascinated by it.

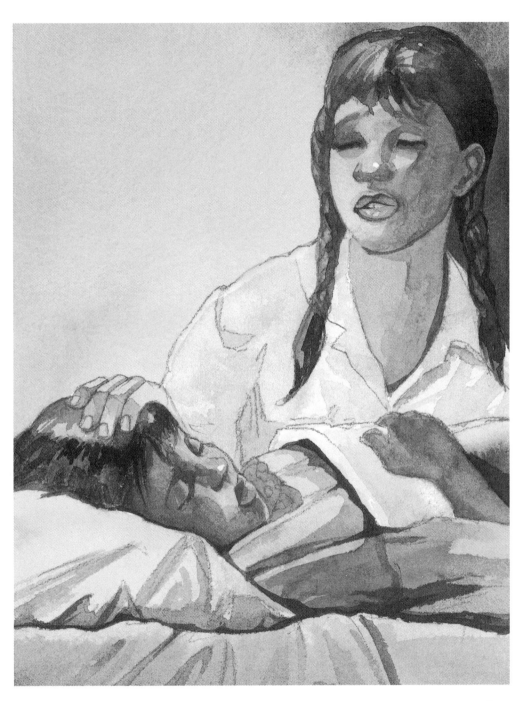

Susan had received sad news one day. Her niece was very, very ill.

Students at work in the dissecting room of the New York Medical College and Hospital for Women in New York City, 1870.

Susan was the first Black woman to attend the Medical College. She was an excellent student. She took classes in biology and chemistry. She learned how different parts of the body worked. She studied plants and how they could be used to treat illnesses.

When her classmates were sleeping, Susan was up studying. She spent long hours at hospitals learning to care for the sick.

On March 23, 1870, Susan graduated. She was the first Black woman to receive a medical degree in New York State, and the third in the United States.

Right away, Dr. Susan Smith opened a doctor's office in her Brooklyn home. In the beginning, business was slow. At first, people did not trust her. But the patients that she had helped told their friends and families about the caring, new doctor. Word about Susan began to spread. After a while, her practice started to grow.

Soon, Susan opened another office in Manhattan. She treated Blacks and Whites.

Fulton Street at City Hall Park was one of Brooklyn's busiest sections in the 1890s. Dr. Susan McKinney Steward opened her first doctor's office in Brooklyn.

She helped the poor and the rich. There were stories about her achievements in newspapers. She was famous.

On July 12, 1871, Susan married Reverend William G. McKinney. They had two children, William and Anna.

Sadly, in 1890 the doctor's husband became ill and died. Three years later, she married Reverend Theophilus Gould Steward, who was the chaplain of the 25th U.S. Colored Infantry. The men of the infantry were also known as Buffalo soldiers. The doctor traveled with her husband to different forts where she treated many Black soldiers.

Throughout her career, Susan worked hard for her patients. She gave lectures to the public about health, nutrition, and medicine. She often spoke about women's rights and the progress of Black women.

In 1881, Susan helped found the Memorial Hospital for Women and Children. She looked after senior citizens at the Brooklyn Home for

Dr. Steward helped provide medical services to Black servicemen known as Buffalo soldiers.

Aged Colored People. She was on the staff of the New York Medical College and Hospital for Women. Susan also belonged to the New York State Homeopathic Medical Society.

The dedicated doctor died on March 7, 1918. She was 71 years old. The Susan Smith McKinney Junior High School, in Brooklyn, New York, was named in her honor on September 25, 1974. Later, the Susan Smith McKinney Steward Medical Society was founded by a group of Black women doctors.

George Washington Carver

BORN ABOUT 1864 - DIED 1943

World-Famous Agricultural Scientist

On a cold, dark night in 1864, a gang of masked White men burst into a slave cabin near Diamond Creek, Missouri. They surrounded a baby named George and his mother, Mary Carver.

"Please, don't hurt my baby!" cried Mary, as she held the sickly boy in her arms. The men ignored her. They were slave raiders—

they kidnapped slaves and sold them in different states. The gang snatched Mary and George and rode off into the night.

Moses Carver, a White slave owner, owned Mary, George, and Jim—George's older brother. Moses sent a man to search for Mary and George. The man found the cold and sick baby boy. But George and Jim never saw their mother again. Moses and his wife, Susan, raised and cared for the boys.

The more George grew, the more curious he became. Young George spent a lot of time outdoors looking at plants. *How do flowers get their color?* George wondered. *What makes plants grow?* This curiosity later helped George Washington Carver become a world-famous agricultural scientist.

Young George was very smart. He grew all sorts of plants in his garden. If they were dying, he made them healthy and strong. "George sure has a way with plants!" everyone said. They called him the "Plant Doctor."

Young George spent a lot of time outdoors caring for plants.

When George turned 12, he left home to go to school. Though slavery had ended in 1865, many schools would not accept Blacks. So George traveled all over Kansas to find Black schools. Kind families took him in while he studied. He washed clothes and cooked to earn his keep.

In 1886, George graduated from Minneapolis High School in Minneapolis, Kansas. He was 22 years old. The next year, George was accepted to study at Simpson College in Indianola, Iowa. George studied art at Simpson. But he was still curious about plant life. So in 1891, he went to Iowa State College of Agriculture in Ames, Iowa. There, George studied plants and farming. He graduated in 1894. He was soon to be Instructor Carver.

For a while he taught at the college and took care of the greenhouse. He continued to do experiments with plants, and he discovered cures for plant diseases. He was encouraged

At Simpson College, young Henry A. Wallace took walks with George Washington Carver and learned about plants and flowers. Wallace later became Secretary of Agriculture for the United States.

by the Wallaces, a prominent family in the community.

One day, George received an important letter from Booker T. Washington. He was the head of the Tuskegee Institute, an all-Black college in Tuskegee, Alabama.

"Would you please come and teach at our school?" asked Booker T. Washington. George happily accepted the invitation for the job of professor. In 1896, he arrived at the institute.

Cotton farms surrounded Tuskegee. After years of planting cotton, the soil was worn out. The farmers were having problems growing their cotton crop. Insects ate up the cotton that did grow. Without cotton, farmers couldn't make a decent living.

George was able to help. He taught his students how to make the soil healthy, and he taught the farmers, too.

"We need to put good things like peanuts into the soil," said George. "Peanuts are healthy and they taste good, too!"

Professor Carver helped Black farmers improve their crops.

The farmers planted peanuts, and just as George said, the soil became healthy. The peanuts grew and grew. Soon there were too many peanuts.

"What are we going to do with all these peanuts?" asked the farmers.

George wasn't sure. So he did many experiments. He found that he could make many things from peanuts. He made oil, soap, and butter—in total, he made over 300 products from peanuts!

Professor Carver's research helped change the way farmers planted their crops all over the South. He was invited to speak about his work with peanuts to the United States Congress.

The professor studied other crops, too. He made 118 products from sweet potatoes—flour, starch, and rubber, to name a few. Because of his research, sweet potatoes and peanuts became the biggest-selling crops in the South.

Soon George was written about in newspapers everywhere. Colleges invited him

SOME PRODUCTS MADE FROM PEANUTS
by George Washington Carver

instant coffee	butter	cocoa
flour	lotion	milk
paints	shampoo	soap
vinegar	cooking oil	glycerin
wood stains	shaving cream	ink

to speak. People sent him money for research. Important businessmen such as Henry Ford (who designed cars) and Thomas Edison (a famous inventor) offered him jobs. But George did not take the jobs. He wanted to teach.

George continued to teach until he was very old.

Professor George Washington Carver died on January 5, 1943. He had taught at the Tuskegee Institute for 47 years.

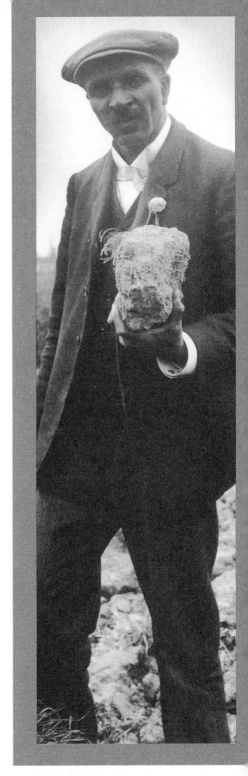

Dr. Carver helped to make soil healthy by growing peanuts.

Ernest Everett Just
BORN 1883 - DIED 1941

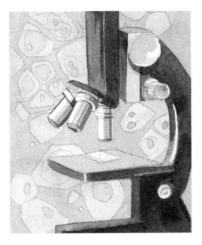

Remarkable Marine Biologist

Ernest Everett Just was born on August 14, 1883, in Charleston, South Carolina. His parents, Charles and Mary, had two younger children, Hunter and Inez.

One day in August 1886, when Ernest was three, there was a terrible earthquake. The earthquake shook Ernest out of bed. Everything crashed around him. Many people in the town were killed. But the Just family survived. In a strange way, the earthquake would help to shape Ernest's life.

Because the quake damaged the Justs' home, they had to move. Mary Just and a group of other Black families bought some land on St. James Island in South Carolina. A town was built on the land. It was called Maryville, after Ernest's mother. Maryville is where Ernest first showed an interest in science. Ernest would grow up to become a well-known scientist of marine biology.

Ernest took long walks through the woods in Maryville. He stared at the flowers and the animals. He was very curious about how all life began. *One day I'll learn more about these things*, thought Ernest. And he did.

He attended schools for Black children. But southern Black schools were not as good as the schools for White children. Mary Just wanted Ernest to have the best education, and the best schools were up north.

Ernest took long walks through the woods in Maryville, South Carolina.

One day Ernest heard about Kimball Academy, a high school in Meridien, New Hampshire. His mother sent a letter to the school applying for a scholarship for Ernest. They waited for an answer. Then Ernest decided to go visit the school instead.

At 17 years of age, Ernest sailed off on a ship to New York. He worked on the ship to pay his fare. "When I reached New York, I had a $5 bill and two pairs of shoes," Ernest later said. When Ernest finally arrived at Kimball Academy, he found out that he had won the scholarship!

Young Ernest was so smart that he finished school in three years instead of four. He graduated in 1903, the top student in his class. He won a scholarship to Dartmouth College in Hanover, New Hampshire.

At Dartmouth College, Ernest took every biology class offered. He was most excited to learn about marine animals, animals that live in the sea. He was an excellent student. Ernest

Ernest Just was a top student at Dartmouth. He graduated with honors.

graduated from Dartmouth with honors in 1907.

After graduation, Ernest looked for a job as a research biologist. But those jobs weren't being offered to Black scientists. Some Whites didn't believe Blacks were good in science. So Ernest took a teaching job at Howard University, an all-Black college in Washington, D.C.

Though he enjoyed teaching, Ernest missed learning about sea animals. Soon he had the chance to do both. In 1909, he began studying at the Marine Biological Laboratory in Woods Hole, Massachusetts. Scientists did research on sea animals there. Ernest taught at Howard in the winter and studied at Woods Hole in the summer. He was 26 years old.

The young scientist did important work at Woods Hole. He studied the egg cells of sea animals. He learned how the eggs fertilized, or developed into living creatures. He discovered

At Woods Hole, Dr. Just studied many different kinds of sea life, including the sea urchin.

which parts of a cell made a creature look the way it did. Other scientists were impressed with Ernest's work. His research appeared in science textbooks and magazines.

Soon Ernest had something different to celebrate. On June 26, 1912, he married Ethel Highwarden, a teacher. They had three children, Margaret, Highwarden, and Maribel.

On February 12, 1915, Ernest Just was honored by the National Association for the Advancement of Colored People (NAACP). This is an organization that fights for the equal rights of minorities. For his work in biology, the NAACP awarded Ernest the Spingarn Medal, a new award for outstanding achievements by a Black American. Ernest was the first to receive the Spingarn. Newspapers carried the big story.

The award-winning scientist kept working and studying. He attended the University of Chicago in Illinois. When he graduated on June 16, 1916, he was a doctor of *zoology*, the study of animal life.

After a while, Dr. Just became known as "the expert" on the early life of sea animals. Dr. Just once challenged the work of a well-known scientist, Dr. Jacques Loeb. Dr. Loeb said he could create new sea animals by adding a chemical to unfertilized eggs in extremely salty seawater. But Dr. Just said he could create new sea animals by simply adding the seawater.

Dr. Just added the seawater to the unfertilized egg cells. Eventually, he looked through his microscope and saw new sea animals swimming around!

Even though Dr. Just had achieved a great deal, prejudice prevented him from getting important jobs in the United States. So by the late 1930s, Dr. Just lived mostly in Europe, studying and working in different laboratories. Scientists there respected his hard work,

Ernest Everett Just was honored by the United States Postal Service. His picture is a part of the Black Heritage Series.

and they didn't treat him badly because he was Black.

Dr. Ernest Just died from cancer on October 27, 1941, in Washington, D.C. He was 58. He wrote over 60 papers and two books about his great work.

Percy Lavon Julian

BORN 1899 - DIED 1975

Outstanding Chemist

One afternoon, Percy Lavon Julian came home from elementary school very excited. "Look, Dad!" Percy cried, waving his math test in the air. Percy had received a grade of 80. "Hmmm," said Mr. Julian. "Next time make it 100, son." Percy never forgot those words.

Young Percy was James and Elizabeth Julian's first child. They had high hopes for him. Hard work and education meant a lot to the Julians.

Percy went to all-Black schools in Montgomery, Alabama. That was the law. Black children and White children weren't allowed to attend school together. And the all-Black schools didn't always provide the best education.

One day, Percy walked to an all-White high school. He climbed up the fence and looked in the school window. He saw students working on chemistry experiments. *I want to do that!* thought Percy. Years later he would become a world-famous chemist.

Percy graduated from high school in 1916. Soon he was boarding a train to DePauw University in Greencastle, Indiana.

College was not easy at first. Percy was the only Black student in the school. Teachers at DePauw said his high school did not prepare him well for college. So Percy had to take high school *and* college classes. Plus, he worked as a shoeshine boy and a waiter.

Nevertheless, Percy studied hard and he

Percy saw students doing experiments. He wanted to study science, too.

did well in his classes. In fact, he received the highest grade in his chemistry class.

In 1920, Percy graduated from DePauw. He was valedictorian, the top student chosen to give a farewell speech to the graduating class. Percy wanted to continue his education. But no university would accept him. So he taught chemistry for a while. Then in 1922, he was accepted to Harvard University in Cambridge, Massachusetts. A year later, he received a master's degree in organic chemistry.

Eventually, Percy traveled to Europe to attend the University of Vienna in Austria. In 1929, he earned a doctor of chemistry degree from the university. Now everyone called him Dr. Julian.

In Vienna, Dr. Julian made an important discovery. He learned that soybeans could have medical uses. He wanted to experiment more with these beans. So he returned to DePauw University to continue his research at the school's laboratory.

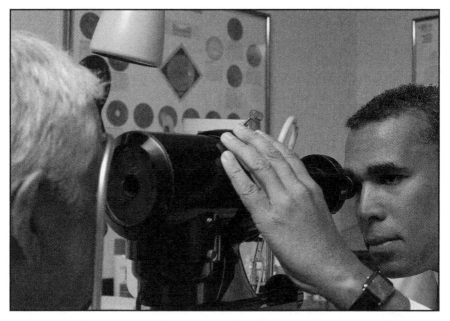

Percy Julian created man-made drugs to fight eye disease.

After many experiments, Percy created a drug that treats *glaucoma*, an eye disease that can cause blindness. Soon, everyone was talking about Dr. Julian and his work. Scientists from all over the world congratulated him. He was so proud. So was Anna Johnson, whom Dr. Julian married on December 24, 1936. They later had two children, Percy Jr. and Faith.

In 1936, Dr. Julian went to work for the Glidden Company. The company made paints and varnishes. Dr. Julian was manager of Fine Chemicals at Glidden. He was also chief chemist and director of research of the Soya Products Division, the Vegetable Oil and Food Division.

While at Glidden, Dr. Julian used the soybean to make many products. He made *Aero-foam*, a chemical that puts out gas and oil fires. This product saved thousands of soldiers' lives in World War II. He also made a new type of *cortisone*, a drug used to treat arthritis pain and other illnesses.

In 1954, Dr. Julian left Glidden to start his own company. It was called Julian Laboratories, Inc. He had an office in Chicago and another in Mexico. Dr. Julian's company was very successful. After six years, he sold his business for millions of dollars.

Dr. Julian received many outstanding awards and honors. He also fought for equal rights for Blacks and women. He organized other Black professionals. Together they

Dr. Julian made a new type of cortisone from the soybean. It was used to treat arthritis pain and other illnesses.

raised money to support the civil rights movement. Dr. Julian wanted to help future generations and build a world where scientists could get jobs based on their skills and not their skin color.

Today, Percy Julian's work in the field of science continues to help many people of all races.

Dr. Julian died on April 19, 1975. In 1990, he was inducted into the Inventors Hall of Fame in Akron, Ohio.

Shirley Ann Jackson

BORN 1946

Great Nuclear Scientist

"**M**om, one day everyone will call me 'Shirley the Great'!" exclaimed four-year-old Shirley Ann Jackson. Mrs. Jackson looked at her young child and smiled.

Shirley was born in Washington, D.C., on August 5, 1946. Her parents, Beatrice and George Jackson, believed their little girl was special, too. They were right. Shirley Ann Jackson achieved many "firsts." She would become one of the most respected nuclear physicists in the United States.

As a young girl, Shirley liked science so much she did experiments at home just for fun! One day Shirley decided to do an experiment with bees. She went into the backyard and sneaked up behind bees that were on the rosebushes. She gently scooped the bees into jars. Altogether, she collected bumblebees, yellow jackets, and wasps.

The young future-scientist put three bees—one of each type—into 30 different glass jars. She stored the jars in a space underneath the porch. Shirley studied how different foods affected the bees. Shirley also studied how the bees got along with one another. She wrote down her results in a notebook. Then she set the bees free.

When she started high school in 1960, Shirley was still doing experiments. Now she entered them in the school's science fairs.

Shirley collected bees and did science experiments for fun!

Shirley attended all-Black Roosevelt High School in Washington, D.C.

The school didn't have a good science lab, so Shirley did her experiments at home. Her hard work paid off. She was a straight-A student. "Here comes The Brain," students said when she passed by.

Shirley graduated from Roosevelt High in the summer of 1964. She had the highest grade average in the class.

In the fall, Shirley went to Massachusetts Institute of Technology (MIT), in Cambridge. They had the best programs in math and science. Shirley wanted to become a scientist. She was one of only a handful of Blacks who went to MIT.

But that didn't stop her from reaching for her goal. She studied hard and she passed all of her tests. In 1968, Shirley graduated with a degree in *physics*, the science of matter and energy.

Dr. Jackson feels that science fairs will encourage young African-Americans to enter careers in science and technology.

After graduation Shirley kept studying at MIT. And in 1973, she received a doctor of physics degree. Shirley was the first Black woman at MIT to receive this important certificate.

Shirley mainly studied *theoretical physics*. That means she used math to figure out how *atoms*, the tiniest bits of matter, work. Shirley is one of the first Black women to specialize in this field of science.

In 1976, Shirley went to work for American Telegraph & Telephone (AT&T) Company in Murray Hill, New Jersey. Her work with atoms helped AT&T design and build *circuits*, paths through which electricity can flow. She helped them design and build *semiconductor lasers*, material that lets electricity run through it. Without these materials you wouldn't be

CD production is possible because of semiconductor research.

able to talk to your friends on the phone long-distance or play your CDs.

Through her work, Shirley met Morris A. Washington. He was a physicist at AT&T, too. Shirley and Morris fell in love and got married. They have one son, Alan.

Throughout her career, Shirley has held many big jobs. She has taught at universities. She served for ten years on the New Jersey Commission on Science and Technology. She received many prestigious awards and honors. In 1995, Shirley received a very special honor. President Bill Clinton named her chairman of the U.S. Nuclear Regulatory Commission (NRC) in Rockville, Maryland. This was another *first*. Shirley Jackson became the Commission's first Black chairperson.

The chairperson's job at the NRC is very, very important. It is to make sure nuclear power plants around the country are safe. The chairperson helps find safe places to store

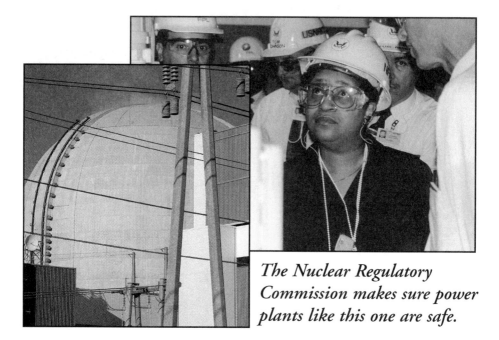

The Nuclear Regulatory Commission makes sure power plants like this one are safe.

harmful nuclear wastes. She makes sure that nuclear wastes are destroyed properly. The chairperson also helps decide how nuclear materials can be used in medical and scientific research.

Dr. Jackson left the NRC in 1999 to accept a position as President of Rensselaer Polytechnic Institute in Schenectady, New York.

Shirley Ann Jackson is proud of her achievements. More than anything, she hopes that her success will inspire other African-American children to become scientists, too.